Withdrawn

Marquis de Lafayette:
Fighting for
America's Freedom

Lisa Colozza Cocca

CRABTREE
Publishing Company
www.crabtreebooks.com

Understanding
The American Revolution

Author: Lisa Colozza Cocca
Publishing plan research and development:
  Sean Charlebois, Reagan Miller
  Crabtree Publishing Company
Editors: Leslie Jenkins, Janet Sweet, Lynn Peppas
Proofreaders: Lisa Slone, Kelly McNiven
Editorial director: Kathy Middleton
Production coordinator: Shivi Sharma
Cover design: Samara Parent, Margaret Amy Salter
Photo research: Nivisha Sinha
Maps: Paul Brinkdopke
Production coordinator and prepress technician: Samara Parent
Print coordinator: Katherine Berti

Written, developed, and produced by Planman Technologies

Cover and Title page (main): *Lafayette's Baptism of Fire* by artist E. Percy Moran. Lafayette is wounded in his first battle in America at the Battle of Brandywine.

Title page (bottom): Three patriots, two playing drums and one playing a fife, lead soldiers into battle.

Photographs and Reproductions
Front cover: Library of Congress (b), Shutterstock (t); Title Page: Library of Congress; Library of Congress; Table of Content: Library of Congress; ©Marion Kaplan / Alamy / IndiaPicture; Library of Congress; Library of Congress; Library of Congress; Ken Riley / The National Guard; Library of Congress; Introduction: Library of Congress; Chapter 1: Library of Congress; Chapter 2: Library of Congress; Chapter 3: Library of Congress; Chapter 4: Library of Congress; Chapter 5: Library of Congress; Chapter 6: Library of Congress; Page 4: Library of Congress; Page 8: Library of Congress; Page 9: ©Marion Kaplan / Alamy / IndiaPicture; Page 10: ©The Art Archive / Alamy / IndiaPicture; Page 11: Library of Congress (t); George Washington Bicentennial Commission / Courtesy National Archives (b); Page 12: Milos Luzanin / Shutterstock; Page 13: Library of Congress; Page 14: Library of Congress; Page 15: Todd Taulman / Shutterstock; Page 16: Hulton Royals Collection / Getty Images (t); Library of Congress (b); Page 17: Library of Congress; Page 18: Danny Smythe / Shutterstock; Page 19: ©Terese Loeb Kreuzer / Alamy / IndiaPicture; Page 20: Library of Congress; Page 21: ©The Art Archive / Alamy / IndiaPicture; Page 22: Yellowj / Shutterstock; Page 23: Library of Congress; Page 24: Library of Congress; Page 25: Library of Congress; Page 26: Library of Congress; Page 28: Library of Congress; Page 31: ©The Art Gallery Collection / Alamy / IndiaPicture; Page 32: Library of Congress; Page 33: Library of Congress; Page 35: Library of Congress; Page 36: Library of Congress; Page 37: Library of Congress (t); Library of Congress (bl); ©Hipix / Alamy / IndiaPicture (br); Page 38: Library of Congress; Page 39: Library of Congress; Page 40: Library of Congress; Page 41: Cynthia Farmer / Shutterstock;
(t = top, b = bottom, l = left, c = center, r = right, bl = bottom left, br = bottom right, bkgd = background, fgd = foreground)

Library and Archives Canada Cataloguing in Publication

Cocca, Lisa Colozza
    Marquis de Lafayette : fighting for America's freedom / Lisa Colozza Cocca.

(Understanding the American Revolution)
Includes bibliographical references and index.
Issued also in electronic format.
ISBN 978-0-7787-0802-5 (bound).--ISBN 978-0-7787-0813-1 (pbk.)

    1. Lafayette, Marie Joseph Paul Yves Roch Gilbert Du Motier, marquis de, 1757-1834--Juvenile literature. 2. United States--History--Revolution, 1775-1783--Participation, French--Juvenile literature. 3. Generals--United States--Biography--Juvenile literature. 4. Statesmen--France--Biography--Juvenile literature. I. Title. II. Series: Understanding the American Revolution (St. Catharines, Ont.)

E207.L2C63 2013   j973.3092   C2013-900240-5

Library of Congress Cataloging-in-Publication Data

CIP available at Library of Congress

Crabtree Publishing Company
www.crabtreebooks.com   1-800-387-7650

Printed in Canada/052014/TT20140331

Published in Canada
Crabtree Publishing
616 Welland Ave.
St. Catharines, Ontario
L2M 5V6

Published in the United States
Crabtree Publishing
PMB 59051
350 Fifth Avenue, 59th Floor
New York, New York 10118

Published in the United Kingdom
Crabtree Publishing
Maritime House
Basin Road North, Hove
BN41 1WR

Published in Australia
Crabtree Publishing
3 Charles Street
Coburg North
VIC 3058

TABLE *of* CONTENTS

Introduction

I n April 1775, war broke out between Great Britain and its **colonies** in America. Tension had been building for years. The colonists were angry about the taxes from Britain. They wanted more say in their government.

The American Revolution

In December 1773, the colonists held a protest known as the Boston Tea Party. Ships carrying tea from Great Britain had landed in Boston Harbor a month earlier. The colonists demanded that the British government remove the tax on the tea. Otherwise, the colonists would send the entire **cargo** of tea back to Britain. Britain refused, so on December 16, a group of colonists slipped down to the docks at night. They boarded the ships and threw the tea in the ocean.

Major Events

1773

December 16
Boston Tea Party

1774

September 5
First Continental Congress

1775

April 19
Battle of Lexington; American Revolution begins

The Boston Tea Party

THE DESTRUCTION OF TEA AT BOSTON HARBOR.

The action angered King George III, the British **monarch**. The British government passed laws that were known as the **Intolerable Acts**. These laws put more restrictions on colonial trade and reduced local governments' power.

> *Taxation and representation are in their nature inseparable; the right of withholding or granting of their money is the only effective security of a free people against the encroachments of despotism and tyranny.*
>
> —George Mason, Fairfax Resolves, July 18, 1774

A Revolution Breaks Out

The colonies reacted to these new laws in the fall of 1774. They formed the First Continental Congress. The **delegates** sent King George a strong message: **repeal** the Intolerable Acts. King George responded by sending troops to control the colonies and take the colonists' weapons. Shots rang out. The war began, and George Washington became the commander of the Continental Army.

The war was long and difficult. The colonists, known as **Patriots**, would not only be fighting the British **Redcoats**, but some of their neighbors, too. Not all of the colonists wanted independence. Some, called **Loyalists**, remained loyal to King George. The Patriots would not be alone, however. Before long, French volunteers joined the Patriots in their struggle. Among the volunteers would be a young **nobleman**, the Marquis de Lafayette.

The Battle of Concord

"By the rude bridge that arched the flood
Their flag to April's breeze unfurled
Here once the embattled farmers stood
And fired the shot heard 'round the world."

—from "Concord Hymn"
by American poet
Ralph Waldo Emerson, 1877

North America before the American Revolution, 1763

*This line shows the farthest west British settlers were allowed to go. The rest of the land was reserved for Native Americans.

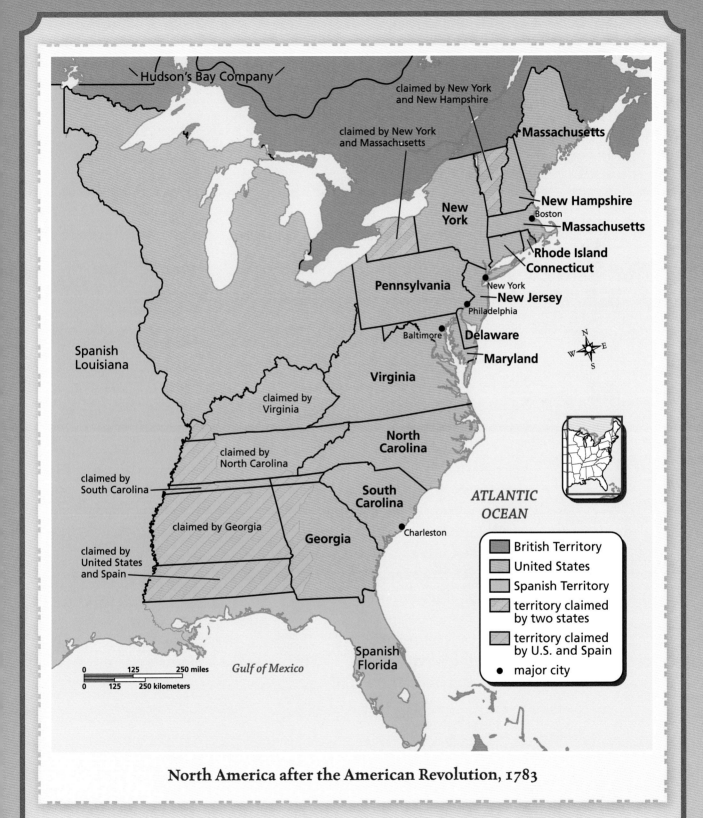

North America after the American Revolution, 1783

Early Years and Influences

Marie-Joseph Paul Yves Roch Gilbert du Motier, the future Marquis de Lafayette and "Hero of Two Worlds" was born on September 6, 1757.

Family

Like his father before him, Gilbert was born at home at the Château de Chavaniac in France. His many names were given as a source of protection. Gilbert—like generations of men in his family—was expected to join the armed services when he grew up. His mother believed that naming him after saints would keep him safe in battle.

His great-grandfather had been a respected soldier who built the family fortune. Gilbert's grandfather was a member of the King's Musketeers. His father was also a military officer. He was a colonel fighting in what would become the **Seven Years' War**. Young Gilbert's life would be shaped by war and his family's involvement in it.

Gilbert as a young man

An Early Loss

Gilbert's father was killed in the Battle of Minden on August 1, 1759. Gilbert was not yet two years old. The battle, one of the largest in the Seven Years' War, pitted the French against the British. Gilbert found out that his father died in battle with British troops under the command of General William Phillips. The loss of his father to British **artillery** would remain with Gilbert forever. It would fuel his need for revenge against Great Britain. Unfortunately, it was only the first of the major losses Gilbert would suffer in childhood.

Growing Up

Shortly after the death of Gilbert's father, his mother left for Paris to join her family. She left young Gilbert in his grandmother's care. Two aunts soon joined the household. Gilbert was allowed to run and play freely. His grandmother was generous to the local **peasants**. She treated them fairly. Her example was a strong influence on Gilbert's developing character.

The Seven Years' War

The Seven Years' War took place from 1756 through 1763. It involved all of the major powers in Europe, North America, Central America, India, the Philippines, and the West Coast of Africa. In the United States, it is most often called the French and Indian War. One of the major causes of the war was the conflict between France and Great Britain over North American colonies.

Château de Chavaniac, Lafayette's birthplace

Paris in the 1760s

Off to Paris

When Gilbert turned ten, his great-grandfather decided it was time for Gilbert to come to Paris. Gilbert was not happy about this. He loved the freedom he had at his grandmother's home. However, his great-grandfather insisted. He believed it was time for Gilbert to start preparing for his future responsibilities. Once in Paris, Gilbert enrolled in school. There he studied the Latin classics along with writing, French, science, philosophy, and religion. At the same time, his great-grandfather added his name to a list of future members of the King's Musketeers. When Gilbert was 12, his mother died. A few weeks later, his great-grandfather died too. Gilbert became a wealthy young orphan. He inherited money and a castle. He also inherited a title. Young Gilbert was now the Marquis de Lafayette.

The Young Officer

Lafayette then followed in his grandfather's footsteps. At the age of 14, he became an officer **cadet** in the Black Musketeers. His fellow cadets, like Lafayette, came from wealthy noble families. They participated in military reviews and prepared for their future.

> "
> *From the time I was eight, I longed for glory.*
>
> —Marquis de Lafayette
> "

A Wedding for Lafayette

In 1772, Lafayette graduated from school. Relatives set out to arrange a marriage for the fifteen year old. They chose a cousin, Marie Adrienne Françoise de Noailles. Adrienne was 14 years old and a member of one of the wealthiest families in France. The marriage would combine the wealth of the two families. This would allow Lafayette to become part of the inner circle at the court of King Louis XVI.

Lafayette moved into his future bride's family home, but the pair did not marry until two years later on April 11, 1774. After the wedding, the couple remained with her parents and siblings.

People in the War

King Louis XVI

King Louis XVI became heir to the throne of France in 1765 when he was ten years old. In 1770, he married Marie Antoinette. He became king at the age of 19 when his grandfather died. In his early reign, he provided religious freedom for the French and support for the Americans in the Revolution. Later, his **economic** choices led his country into near **bankruptcy**. He made many cutbacks, which angered the nobles and the people. Meanwhile, he and his queen continued to enjoy a royal life. He was eventually convicted of **treason** during the French Revolution. He was executed on January 21, 1793.

Adrienne de Noailles, wife of the Marquis de Lafayette

Lieutenant Lafayette

A year later, Lafayette was serving as a second lieutenant in a **regiment**, the Noailles Dragoons. He served under the command of his uncle, the Marquis de Noailles. His military career had begun. It was his first step toward becoming the "hero of two worlds."

The Freemasons

In late spring of 1775, Lafayette went to his annual military training session. He met Charles-François, Comte de Broglie there. Broglie was the commander of Napoleon's Army of the East. He was also the grand master of a traveling military lodge of the **Freemasons**. The Freemasons were a social group, but they also often discussed matters of **equality** and **civil rights**. These were **radical** ideas in a country ruled by a monarch.

Why was Lafayette called the *Hero of Two Worlds*?

In the United States, Lafayette was considered a hero for his courage and skill in battle. Additionally, he was admired for the work he did to get financial and military help for the Patriots. At home in France, he was also considered a hero for his work in the American Revolution. More importantly to the French, Lafayette was admired for the work he did to strengthen the friendship between the two nations and to bring rights to the French **commoners**.

A stamp with the Freemason seal. The seal shows a square ruler and a compass, tools used by architects that are important to the Freemasons.

Becoming a Mason

Broglie realized Lafayette had great wealth and many powerful connections. He invited Lafayette and a few of the young officer's friends to a meeting. The idea of being part of a brotherhood appealed to Lafayette. The meeting began his association with the Masonic Lodge. It also fed Lafayette's growing concern for the rights of others. In particular, the members discussed the struggle of the American colonists.

The Freemasons supported the Patriots' efforts because they believed that freedom and independence were honorable causes. They also liked the fact that the colonists were fighting against Great Britain. Many Frenchmen still resented Great Britain for its role in the Seven Years' War.

Lafayette fought for the Patriot cause after discussing it at the Masonic Lodge.

> *Freemasonry is an order whose leading star is philanthropy and whose principles inculcate an unceasing devotion to the cause of virtue and morality.*
>
> —Marquis de Lafayette

Joining the Revolution

Major Events

1776

July 4
Declaration of Independence

September
Silas Deane is sent to France as a commissioner

1777

Spring
La Victoire sets sail

June
Lafayette arrives in North Carolina

July
Lafayette becomes youngest Major General in the Continental Army

L afayette supported much of what he heard at the Freemason meetings and decided to join the cause.

Lafayette and the American Cause

On August 8, 1775, Lafayette's general interest turned into a desire to join the American Patriots. That evening, the Duke of Gloucester dined with the Freemasons. He spoke about the situation in the colonies. He admired them for fighting for their rights and independence. Lafayette was moved by the duke's passion for the American cause.

At the meetings, Lafayette learned that some of the American leaders were also Freemasons. Lafayette liked the idea that he was in a brotherhood with George Washington and Benjamin Franklin. Soon, news of the Declaration of Independence reached France. Lafayette, like many other Frenchmen, decided it was time to offer more than words. He wanted to go to America to fight in the Continental Army. So in December 1776, Lafayette made plans to go. He would help the American cause and perhaps earn the glory he had dreamed of since childhood.

Washington as a Freemason

14

"

When in the Course of human events, it becomes necessary for one people to dissolve the political bands which have connected them with another, and to assume among the powers of the earth, the separate and equal station to which the Laws of Nature and of Nature's God entitle them, a decent respect to the opinions of mankind requires that they should declare the causes which impel them to the separation.

We hold these truths to be self-evident, that all men are created equal, that they are endowed by their Creator with certain unalienable Rights, that among these are Life, Liberty and the pursuit of Happiness.—That to secure these rights, Governments are instituted among Men, deriving their just powers from the consent of the governed, —That whenever any Form of Government becomes destructive of these ends, it is the Right of the People to alter or to abolish it, and to institute new Government, laying its foundation on such principles and organizing its powers in such form, as to them shall seem most likely to effect their Safety and Happiness. . . . We, therefore, the Representatives of the united States of America, in General Congress, Assembled, do, in the Name, and by Authority of the good People of these Colonies, solemnly publish and declare, That these United Colonies are, and of Right ought to be Free and Independent States. . . . And for the support of this Declaration, with a firm reliance on the protection of divine Providence, we mutually pledge to each other our Lives, our Fortunes and our sacred Honor.

—*from the* Declaration of Independence, *July 4, 1776*

Declaration of Independence

"

People in the War

Duke of Gloucester

Prince William, the younger brother of King George III, was also called the Duke of Gloucester. While the king fought to keep control over the colonies, the duke spoke out in support of the colonists' cause. He traveled to France to stir up support there for the Continental Army.

Secret Plans

Lafayette knew his father-in-law and wife might not be as excited as Lafayette was about his going to America. In fact, he was sure his father-in-law might stop him. He would need to keep his plans secret from them for a while.

Royal Disapproval

He also knew King Louis XVI would likely not approve of his plans. The king had been secretly helping the Americans, but he did not think it would be wise for France to openly support a group fighting against Great Britain. Lafayette was from a wealthy, prominent French family. If Lafayette joined the American forces, it could draw attention to France's involvement in the war.

Baron de Kalb introducing Lafayette to Silas Deane

Making Connections

None of this opposition squashed Lafayette's dreams of fighting with the American Patriots. He decided instead to speak to his friend, the Comte de Broglie, about his idea. Broglie then introduced Lafayette to the Baron Johan de Kalb.

Silas Deane, Congressional Agent

Kalb, in turn, introduced Lafayette to an American, Silas Deane. Deane was in France representing the interests of the Continental Army. Although his purpose was to gain money and goods for the cause, he went beyond the task the Continental Congress had given him.

Many soldiers in France were out of work. France was not actively in conflict with anyone. The French government had reorganized the military and had **disbanded** some of the smaller family regiments. Deane saw this as an opportunity to pull French officers into service to America. Before long, he had an **abundance** of volunteers. Among them was the Marquis de Lafayette.

> "
> *I have a levee of officers and others every morning as numerous, if not as splendid, as a prime minister. Indeed I have had occasionally dukes, generals, and marqueses and even bishops and counts and chevaliers without number, all of whom are jealous, being out of employ here, or having friends they wish to advance in cause of liberty. . . .*
>
> —Silas Deane, in a letter to John Jay, December 2, 1776
> "

People in the War

Silas Deane

Silas Deane was a Connecticut lawyer. The Continental Congress appointed him to be a commissioner to France in September 1776. Deane promised French soldiers high commissions in the Continental Army for their service. He later took part in a plot to remove George Washington as the commander in chief of the Continental Army.

Word Spreads

Lafayette was able to keep his preparations for the trip a secret from his wife and family. Unfortunately, he was not able to keep it a secret from the world. News of young nobles from well-known families joining the American forces created problems for France.

King Louis XVI wanted to avoid another direct conflict with Britain. France **temporarily** blocked American ships from French ports. It also banned the sale of goods to the colonists. In addition, the government threatened to arrest any French soldier who claimed the government ordered them to serve for the colonies. None of this caused Lafayette to change his mind. He was determined to go to America and fight.

A barrel for holding gunpowder

Setting Sail for America

Lafayette told Deane he would buy his own ship for passage to America. Deane saw this as a sign that Lafayette was serious about joining the cause. In return, he promised Lafayette a **commission** as major general in the Continental Army. Lafayette was now more certain than ever he belonged with the Americans.

In the spring of 1777, the merchant ship *La Victoire* set sail for America. Lafayette and a small group of French officers were on board. Lafayette fought seasickness during the 56 days at sea. He spent his time learning some English phrases. He also studied military tactics. Although the nineteen-year-old had been educated to become a soldier, he had never been in battle before.

> "My dear Heart: . . . how will you have taken my going? Do you love me less? Have you forgiven me? . . . I shan't send you a diary of the voyage; days follow each other and are all alike; always sea and sky and the next day just the same . . . [A]s a defender of liberty, which I adore . . . coming to my services to this interesting republic, I am bringing nothing but my good will."
>
> —*Marquis de Lafayette in a letter to his wife Adrienne from aboard* La Victoire, *1777*

This American ship built in 1797 is similar to *La Victoire*, the ship which carried the Marquis de Lafayette to the American colonies.

America!

In June 1777, the ship reached port in South Carolina. The officers were still a long way from their destination of Philadelphia. Lafayette and the other men would have to travel the rest of the way by land. Lafayette bought horses and carriages for the trip. This means of transportation worked well in a city, like Paris, but the route they would follow had different **terrain**. The men would have to travel along rough roads and through swamps. City carriages were not built to handle these challenges. Along the 900-mile (1500-kilometer) trip, the carriages were destroyed. The men continued on horseback. Finally in July, Lafayette and the men reached Philadelphia.

It was time for Lafayette to present himself to Congress. He did not receive the welcome there that he expected. Deane had worked without Congress' approval when he had promised Lafayette a commission. In fact, Deane had promised many French officers high commissions in the Continental Army. Congress did not feel required to fulfill those promises. Lafayette did not give up. He offered to work without **compensation** in any role Congress saw fit to give him. The representatives accepted his offer. They gave him the title he had been promised. This made Lafayette the youngest major general in the Continental Army.

A horse-drawn carriage

Lafayette in Battle

I t did not take long for Lafayette to get his first real war experience. In the fall of 1777, Lafayette fought with George Washington's troops at the Battle of Brandywine.

Wounded and Honored

On September 11, Lafayette was wounded in battle. Washington had his own doctor attend to Lafayette's wounded leg. He then sent Lafayette back to Philadelphia by ship. He wanted Lafayette to remain in the hospital there until his wound healed.

In the meantime, Washington sent a letter about Lafayette to Congress. He praised his work at Brandywine. He gave him credit for saving many other soldiers' lives. When Lafayette was ready to return to service, Congress showed its appreciation for his contributions in battle. It gave him command over a military division from Virginia. At the age of 20, Lafayette had command of 2,200 men.

Major Events

1777
September 11
Lafayette wounded at Battle of Brandywine

1778
May 20
Battle of Barren Hill

June 28
Battle of Monmouth

1780
Late September
Benedict Arnold disappears

1781
Battle of Yorktown

Lafayette wounded at Brandywine

"I shall begin by telling you I am well, because I must end by telling you that we fought in earnest yesterday, and we are not the victors. Our Americans, after holding firm for a considerable time, were finally routed. While I was trying to rally them, the English honored me with a musket shot, which wounded me slightly in the leg...."

—*Marquis de Lafayette in a letter to his wife, Adrienne*

The Soldier's Friend

Supplies were scarce for the soldiers. They often lacked blankets, shoes, warm clothing, and adequate food. Lafayette fought for more supplies for his men. Often he bought the supplies with his own money. During war, officers usually lived in finer **quarters** than the enlisted men and had plentiful food. Lafayette, however, chose to live as his men did. He stayed with the soldiers, ate the same food, and suffered the same problems as the **enlisted** men. This earned him another title, that of "the soldier's friend."

Money Trouble

At home, Lafayette's family worried about the amount of money he was spending. Lafayette had planned to send *La Victoire* back to France to be sold. He then would use the profit to finance his time in America. The ship, however, sank on the way back. Lafayette started drawing on family money. Then his father-in-law put Lafayette on a strict allowance. This forced Lafayette to sign loans against his property.

Military Talent

On May 20, 1778, Lafayette had another chance to show his skills as a military leader. His troops were camped on Barren Hill. Washington sent orders not to remain there for a second night. Lafayette ignored these orders. Staying a second night gave the British troops time to catch up to them. The British heavily outnumbered Lafayette's men and surrounded them on three sides. However, Lafayette arranged his men to retreat in a way that tricked the British into thinking there were more American soldiers than there really were. The Americans were able to escape to safety over the river. Despite the fact he failed to follow orders or complete his mission, Lafayette was praised for his brilliant retreat.

The next month, Lafayette took part in the Battle of Monmouth on June 28, 1778. The Americans fought against the Redcoats from dawn till dusk. It was the biggest battle fought in the north. Neither side won, but the Americans proved something at Monmouth. They showed they were equals to the British in battle. Once again, Lafayette showed his bravery in battle. He earned more admiration from Washington.

People in the War

Molly Pitcher

Molly Pitcher was a nickname of Mary Hays McCauly, who fought in the Battle of Monmouth. Molly was carrying water for the cannons during the battle when her husband was wounded. Molly took up her husband's place at the cannon, helping the Patriots win the battle. She was so important that "Molly Pitcher" has come to be a nickname for all of the women who fought for the Patriots in the American Revolution.

Molly Pitcher at the Battle of Monmouth

Lafayette and Washington

The Conway Plot

Late in 1777, a small group of men tried to get Congress to remove Washington as the commander in chief of the Continental Army. Brigadier General Thomas Conway was the leader of the plot. Conway befriended Lafayette. He tried to get Lafayette to cooperate with the scheme. Although Lafayette admired Conway's military skills, he was dedicated to Washington. In the end, the men were not successful. Congress supported Washington. When Lafayette realized what Conway and his men had tried to do, he worried that Washington would think he had been a part of it. On December 29, 1777, Lafayette wrote Washington the following letter:

"My dear general, I don't need to tell you how I am sorry for all what happens since some time. It is a necessary dependence [part] of my most tender and respectful friendship for you, which affection is . . . much stronger than a so new acquaintance [friendship] seems to admit. But an other reason to be concerned in the present circumstances is my ardent [sincere], and perhaps enthusiastic wishes for the happiness and liberty of this country. I see plainly that America can defend herself if proper measures are taken and now I begin to fear that she could be lost by herself and her own sons. . . . Take away for an instant that modest diffidence [lack of confidence] of yourself . . . you shall see very plainly that if you were lost for America, there is nobody who could keep the army and the revolution for six months. . . . I am now fixed to your fate and I shall follow it and sustain it as well by my sword as by all means in my power. . . ."
—*Marquis de Lafayette to General George Washington, December 29, 1777*

Soldier and Diplomat

In the spring of 1778, Washington made Lafayette his Chief of Foreign Affairs. In this role, Lafayette increased his attempts to gain support from France. He was successful in his efforts. France agreed to send troops and more financial aid. The Count de Rochambeau was given command over the French troops.

In 1779, Lafayette petitioned Congress for a **furlough**. When it was granted, he returned to France briefly. There he negotiated for more troops and for some naval support. This naval support was much needed later in the war.

While Lafayette was in France, he visited with his family. He knew he needed the king's forgiveness for having joined the Americans without permission. The king required Lafayette to remain in **exile** in a hotel, where he would see no one but his family for eight days. After Lafayette's exile ended, the king welcomed him at court. He congratulated Lafayette on his service to the United States.

Lafayette fought bravely for the Patriots. His service was rewarded in France. Lafayette is shown here in the National Guard of France uniform.

Patriotism and Treason

By September 1780, Lafayette was back in America. He accompanied Washington on a trip to West Point. Benedict Arnold was in command there. When Arnold realized Washington was about to learn he was a **traitor**, he disappeared. Lafayette, who admired the patriotism of the colonists, was shaken by Arnold's betrayal of the Patriot cause.

"I cannot describe to you, M. le Chevalier, to what degree I am astounded by this piece of news. . . that an Arnold, a man who . . . had nevertheless, given proof of talent, of patriotism, and especially of the most brilliant courage, should at once destroy his very existence and should sell his country to the tyrants whom he had fought against with glory is an event, M. le Chevalier, which confounds and distresses me, and if I must confess it, humiliates me to a degree that I cannot express. I would give anything in the world if Arnold had not shared our labors with us, and if this man, who it still pains me to call a scoundrel, had not shed his blood in the American cause."

—*Marquis de Lafayette, in a letter to Chevalier de la Luzerne*

Benedict Arnold, shown here giving away Patriot secrets, was caught and tried for treason in a court martial. The Marquis de Lafayette was one of the jurors in the court.

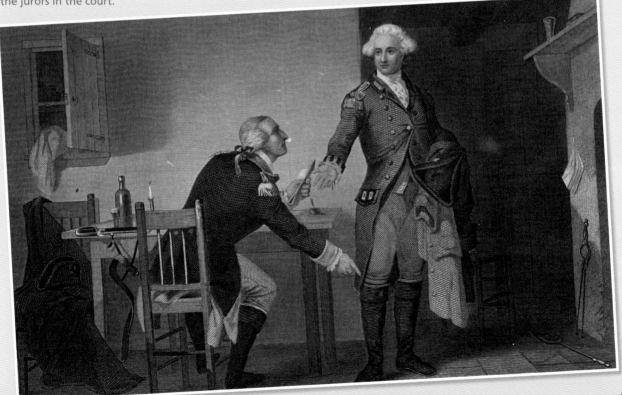

> *" . . . [T]he enemy carried two advanced **redoubts** by storm. . . . The safety of the place is, therefore, so **precarious** that I cannot recommend that the fleet and army should run great risk in endeavouring to save us.*
>
> —Lord Cornwallis, in a letter to Sir Henry Clinton, October 15, 1781 *"*

The Battle of Yorktown

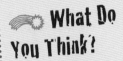

What Do You Think?

How would the American Revolution have been different without French aid to the Patriots?

The final major campaign in the war took place in Yorktown. Lafayette was in the thick of it. Lord Cornwallis' British troops had been weakened by the battles and **skirmishes** in the south. They headed to Virginia to await support and supplies. Cornwallis led his troops to the Yorktown **peninsula**. He believed this position would allow British ships to provide his troops with reinforcements. This proved to be a fatal decision for the British efforts.

The French naval ships that Lafayette had secured created a **blockade** around the Yorktown ports. The British ships could not get through with the support Cornwallis needed. French troops blocked Cornwallis' men to the west. American troops blocked the British from the east. Cornwallis' men remained trapped in this triangle for several days. On October 19, 1781, the British **surrendered** to the Americans at Yorktown.

Peace at Last

Lafayette was greatly praised for his part in the Battle of Yorktown. Not only was he effective on the battleground, but his success at getting the French involved was extremely important. A newspaper report in 1781 summed up public opinion on Yorktown: "The general who contributed most to the success of this great enterprise is without contradiction the Marquis de Lafayette. . . ."

A **peace treaty** would not be signed for another two years after the Battle of Yorktown. Everyone agreed, however, that America had won the war. With no more battles to fight in America, Lafayette asked Congress for another leave of absence. Congress approved, and Lafayette made plans to return to France.

> *" The play, sir, is over.*
>
> —Marquis de Lafayette, after the British surrendered to the Americans, October 1781 *"*

A Lasting Friendship

Lafayette and Washington had become friends immediately. This friendship grew stronger over time. Washington often asked others to treat Lafayette as if he were Washington's own son. Now there would be an ocean between them. Before Lafayette sailed for France, Washington wrote: "I owe it to your friendship and to my affectionate regard for you, my dear Marquis, not to let you leave this country without carrying with you fresh marks of my attachment to you, and new expressions of the high sense I entertain of your military conduct and other important services in the course of the last campaign, although the latter are too well known to need the testimony of my approbation [approval]."

Lafayette responded: "Adieu, my dear General; I know your heart so well that I am sure that no distance can alter your attachment to me. With the same candour I assure that my love, respect, my gratitude for you, are above expression; that, at the moment of leaving you, I felt more than ever the strength of those friendly ties that forever bind me to you."

George Washington presented a watch to the Marquis de Lafayette to celebrate the surrender of Cornwallis at Yorktown.

A Triumphant Return to France

The friendship between Washington and Lafayette continued after Lafayette returned to France. The men wrote to each other often. Lafayette was received in France not only as a hero to America, but also as a hero to France. His work during the American Revolution had strengthened the relationship between France and America.

Representative Government

Lafayette settled in Paris and worked to spread the principles of a **representative government** among the French. He also continued to work to support American interests in France. He helped open the French markets to the New England fisheries. He also helped convince the French government to postpone collection of the first payments of American debt.

Lafayette and Jefferson Work Together

Thomas Jefferson had replaced Benjamin Franklin as ambassador to France in 1784. Lafayette and Jefferson often spoke and worked together. When Lafayette wrote the *Declaration of the Rights of Man and of the Citizen* in 1789, he turned to Jefferson for advice. The document expressed the ideas behind the French Revolution, also known as the *Revolution of 1789*. The newly formed National Assembly approved the declaration on August 26.

Major Events

1782
Lafayette returns to France

1789
Lafayette writes the *Declaration of the Rights of Man and of the Citizen*; French Revolution begins; Lafayette becomes Commander of the National Guard

1792
French Assembly declares war on Austria; King Louis XVI is removed from rule; Lafayette is impeached and later imprisoned

1794
Adrienne is imprisoned

1795
Adrienne is released

1797
Lafayette is released

"

When I was stationed in his country for the purpose of cementing its friendship with ours, and of advancing our mutual interests, this friend of both, was my most powerful auxiliary and advocate. He made our cause his own, as in truth it was that of his native country also. His influence and connections there were great. All doors of all departments were open to him at all times. In truth, I only held the nail, he drove it.

—Thomas Jefferson on Marquis de Lafayette

"

DECLARATION OF THE RIGHTS OF MAN AND OF THE CITIZEN

1. Men are born and remain free and equal in rights. Social distinctions may be founded only upon the general good.
2. The aim of all political association is the preservation of the natural and imprescriptible rights of man. These rights are liberty, property, security, and resistance to oppression.
3. The principle of all sovereignty resides essentially in the nation. No body nor individual may exercise any authority which does not proceed directly from the nation.
4. Liberty consists in the freedom to do everything which injures no one else; hence the exercise of the natural rights of each man has no limits except those which assure to the other members of the society the enjoyment of the same rights. These limits can only be determined by law.
5. Law can only prohibit such actions as are hurtful to society. Nothing may be prevented which is not forbidden by law, and no one may be forced to do anything not provided for by law.
6. Law is the expression of the general will. Every citizen has a right to participate personally, or through his representative, in its foundation. It must be the same for all, whether it protects or punishes. All citizens, being equal in the eyes of the law, are equally eligible to all dignities and to all public positions and occupations, according to their abilities, and without distinction except that of their virtues and talents.

7. No person shall be accused, arrested, or imprisoned except in the cases and according to the forms prescribed by law. Any one soliciting, transmitting, executing, or causing to be executed, any arbitrary [without cause] order, shall be punished. But any citizen summoned or arrested in virtue of the law shall submit without delay, as resistance constitutes an offense.

8. The law shall provide for such punishments only as are strictly and obviously necessary, and no one shall suffer punishment except it be legally inflicted in virtue of a law passed and promulgated before the commission of the offense.

9. As all persons are held innocent until they shall have been declared guilty, if arrest shall be deemed indispensable, all harshness not essential to the securing of the prisoner's person shall be severely repressed by law.

10. No one shall be disquieted on account of his opinions, including his religious views, provided their manifestation does not disturb the public order established by law.

—from the Declaration of the Rights of Man and of the Citizen, *1789*

An oil painting outlining the *Declaration of the Rights of Man and of the Citizen* painted in 1789.

What Do You Know!

After the Revolution of 1789, France was under the "Reign of Terror." It began on September 5, 1793, when Maximilien Robespierre declared terror "the order of the day." Robespierre was the head of the Committee of Public Safety during the early French Revolution. Over the next ten months, between 18,000 and 40,000 people were executed in France by guillotine. Robespierre saw the Reign of Terror as a necessity. It would rid France of all opposition to the Revolution. It ended on July 27, 1794. On that day, Robespierre was executed for crimes against the French Republic.

The National Guard

The National Assembly appointed Lafayette the Commandant of the National Guard. Instead of making war, his job was to keep peace. This was not an easy task. The American Revolution had taken a toll on the French economy. Many of the French commoners lacked the basics in life, such as enough food. Riots and fights often broke out.

Tension in France

As anger among the people grew, more and more threats were made against the king and queen. Leopold II was the Emperor of Austria. He was also the brother of Marie Antoinette, the Queen of France. He did not want the monarchy in France to be overthrown. War soon broke out between France and Austria.

No Longer Safe in France

Lafayette remained a supporter of King Louis XVI. After the National Assembly **deposed** the king in August 1792, they **impeached** Lafayette. He was declared a traitor and sentenced to death. Lafayette and his family were not safe in Paris without the protection of the National Guard. They returned to Chavaniac and made plans to leave the country.

The French Revolution

A Failed Escape

Lafayette started his escape from France through the Netherlands. He was captured by the Austrians. Lafayette claimed to be an American citizen and asked to be brought to the American consulate. The Austrians refused. They saw Lafayette as a French revolutionist. After all, he had written the *Declaration of the Rights of Man and of the Citizen.* The document had stirred trouble among the commoners who wanted the rights it proposed.

> " *I wanted to go die in Paris. But I feared that such an example of popular ingratitude would only discourage future promoters of liberty. So I left.*
>
> —Marquis de Lafayette "

Prisoner Lafayette

Lafayette was taken to prison. He spent his days alone in a cell. Back in France, his family's property was taken by the new French government. His wife, Adrienne, took up his cause. She sent their son, Georges Washington—named after President Washington—into hiding. In June 1794, Adrienne was jailed for speaking out against the government. Their daughters, Anastasie and Virginie, were placed under house arrest.

Lafayette in prison

Help from America

The Lafayettes were not forgotten by Americans. Many, including George Washington, tried to negotiate Lafayette's release from prison. American minister to France James Monroe and his wife often visited Adrienne in prison. They wanted to bring the world's attention to the situation. They hoped this would embarrass the French government and cause them to release her. On January 22, 1795, Adrienne was freed.

🕊 What Do You Think?

How would James Monroe's prison visits to Lafayette's wife embarrass the French government?

Wretched Conditions

Before Adrienne and her daughters fled to America, Adrienne got permission to visit her husband in prison. She found him living in terrible conditions. Adrienne refused to leave him there. She and their daughters moved into the cell next to his. She wrote to friends about the conditions. This created an international **stir**. When Adrienne became sick, the Austrians received even more pressure to release Lafayette.

Free Again

On October 4, 1797, Napoleon Bonaparte negotiated Lafayette's release after five years in prison. Lafayette remained in exile in Holland and Germany until 1799. When he returned to France, Bonaparte offered Lafayette several positions and honors, including Ambassador to the United States. Lafayette refused them all. He did not believe Bonaparte's government was truly representative.

Bonaparte did not forget or forgive Lafayette's refusal to support him. When word of George Washington's death reached France, Bonaparte planned a memorial service. Lafayette was not invited. Bonaparte ordered there to be no mention of Lafayette in any of the speeches at the event.

> *If Bonaparte had been willing to serve the cause of liberty, I should have been devoted to him. But I can neither approve of an arbitrary government, nor associate myself with it.*
>
> —Marquis de Lafayette

A Return to Public Life

Lafayette maintained the life of a **gentleman farmer** throughout the rest of Bonaparte's reign. When the French monarchy was restored, Lafayette returned to public service. In 1818, he was elected to the Chamber of Deputies. His new job consisted mainly of letters, speeches, and meetings. However, Lafayette also cooperated with a plan to overthrow the French monarchy. The plot failed and Lafayette was removed from his position in 1824.

Back Pay

When Lafayette's property was **seized** by the French government, his American friends were worried. Thomas Jefferson suggested Congress vote to **retroactively** reject Lafayette's offer to fight for the Americans without compensation. Then they could **appropriate** his back pay. Washington supported this idea and Congress agreed. In March 1794, they granted him $24,424. Later, the American government provided him with more money and land in America.

5 An Invitation to America

I n honor of the fiftieth anniversary of the Revolutionary War, Lafayette was invited to tour the country he fought to found.

Return to America

After being relieved of his duties at the Chamber of Deputies, Lafayette received an invitation from President John Monroe and the United States Congress. The fiftieth anniversary of the start of the American Revolution was soon approaching. Lafayette was the only surviving major general from the American Revolution. Monroe and Congress wanted Lafayette to visit the United States. Lafayette accepted their invitation.

Lafayette thought the trip might also help the French see how a true republic worked. He brought along his secretary, Auguste Levasseur. It was Levasseur's job to send reports of the trip back to France. In 1828, Levasseur published a book about the trip.

Major Events

1824

August 15
Lafayette arrives in Staten Island

August 24
Lafayette visits Boston

September 28
Lafayette visits Philadelphia

October 2
Lafayette visits Washington, D.C.

October 17
Lafayette visits Mount Vernon

1825

May 3
Lafayette visits Nashville

July 26
Lafayette visits Brandywine

September 8
Lafayette departs for France

Lafayette greets troops in New York. The troops later took the name "National Guards" in honor of Lafayette's force in France.

The Celebration Begins

On August 15, 1824, Lafayette arrived in Staten Island, New York. It was the start of his year-long tour. Along the way he visited Boston, Philadelphia, Baltimore, and Washington, D.C. He took part in the anniversary celebrations at Yorktown that October. In November, he visited Monticello. He enjoyed visiting with Thomas Jefferson there.

"Mr. Jefferson received me with strong emotion. I found him much aged, without doubt, after a separation of thirty-five years, but bearing marvelously well under his eighty one years of age, in full possession of all the vigor of his mind and heart which he has consecrated to the building of a good and fine university. . . . Today [November 8] we visited this beautiful institution which occupies the honored old age of our illustrious friend. His daughter Mrs. Randolph lives with him; he is surrounded by a large family and his house is admirably located. We attended a public banquet in Charlottesville, [Mrs.] Jefferson and [Mrs.] Madison were with us."
—*Marquis de Lafayette's account of visiting Thomas Jefferson at Monticello*

The Marquis de Lafayette visiting Mount Vernon, George Washington's home in Virginia

A Hero's Welcome

From Monticello, Lafayette returned to Washington, D.C. He spent most of the winter there attending events and receptions. At the end of February, Lafayette was back on the road. He visited New Orleans, St. Louis, Nashville, Louisville, Cincinnati, Pittsburgh, and Buffalo. He made stops in many small towns and at many American battlefields. Everywhere he went, he received a warm and enthusiastic reception.

A Bonus for Business

Lafayette's visit had some unexpected bonuses for America. One was the boost it gave to the economy. Souvenirs of Lafayette's visit sold in large volumes. American craftsmen produced glass, ceramic, wood, and textile items with Lafayette's image on them.

It seemed that Americans could not get their fill of news about the major general. Newspapers were filled with accounts of Lafayette's trip. Several biographies of Lafayette were published. These goods, along with his speeches, helped strengthen America's identity as a republic.

Lafayette's visit created a swell in the American arts. Numerous paintings, sculptures, and engravings of Lafayette showed the talents of American artists. Musicians, poets, and orators produced songs, poems, and speeches that shared the story of Lafayette.

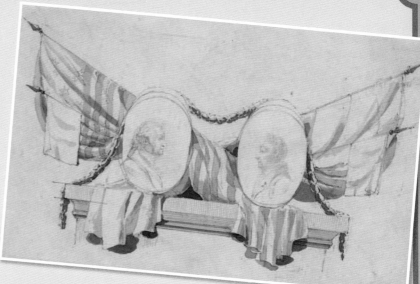

Lafayette memorabilia

Homeward Bound

After a few more months of touring, it was time for Lafayette to return to France. On September 8, 1825, the "hero of two worlds" boarded a ship to go home. The new frigate was christened *Brandywine*, in honor of Lafayette's first time in battle.

🌠 What Do You Think?

How was Lafayette both a hero to the French people and a problem for the French government?

6

Death of a Hero

Lafayette's death was mourned by people around the world, particularly in the United States.

What Do You Know!

More than half of the states in the United States have one or more cities or counties named for Lafayette. Some of the most common names are Lafayette, Fayette, Fayetteville, and LaGrange (named for Lafayette's summer home).

Death and Burial

Lafayette died on May 20, 1834. He had never achieved his dream of establishing a truly representative French republic. People in France and in the United States reacted differently to his death. In France, the government did not allow a public funeral. Reports of the American tour had boosted Lafayette's political position in France. The leaders were afraid a public display would cause demonstrations against the government. Instead, Lafayette was buried under guard in Picpus Cemetery in Paris. His grave was covered with American soil.

Tributes to a Hero

In the United States, his death was recognized publicly. It was another chance for Americans to thank Lafayette for his contributions to the nation. John Quincy Adams gave a **eulogy** for Lafayette before both houses of Congress. It lasted three hours. President Jackson declared a national time of mourning. Americans continued to honor Lafayette long after the mourning period ended. Many of these honors became permanent reminders of Lafayette. States named towns and counties for him, such as Fayette County in Pennsylvania. There are more places in the United States named for him than any other foreign person.

Lafayette as an older man before his death in 1834

The Armed Forces Pay Tribute

During World War I, the Americans and French were allies. American pilots flew side by side with French pilots. The Americans wanted to honor Lafayette's contributions to America. They named their Air Force squadron the "Lafayette Escadrille."

World War I also gave Americans a chance to right an old wrong. No Americans had been present at Lafayette's burial. General John Pershing brought a large military group to Lafayette's gravesite. They flew an American flag over the grave. An American flag has always flown over the grave of Lafayette since then.

The Lafayette Escadrille

Lafayette statue in Prospect Park, Brooklyn, New York

Across America

Statues of Lafayette can be found across the country. They stand in public parks, gardens, and buildings. Many were made with private funding. For example, Henry Harteau, a Brooklyn businessman, wanted to honor the memory of Lafayette. He left $35,000 in his will in 1895 to be used to build a memorial to America's "adopted son." The money was used to build a 19-foot (6-meter) tall bronze and granite sculpture of Lafayette. It stands in Prospect Park in Brooklyn, New York. The statue was based on a painting, "Lafayette at Yorktown" by Jean-Baptiste Le Paon.

THE MARQUIS DE LAFAYETTE

"This monument was erected and presented by Henry Harteau, a distinguished citizen of Brooklyn, to be an enduring tribute to the memory of one who as a friend and companion of the immortal Washington fought to establish in our country those vital principles of liberty and human brotherhood which he afterward labored to establish in his own."

—*Inscription on "The Marquis de Lafayette" in Prospect Park, Brooklyn*

Lafayette College

One significant tribute to the "hero of two worlds" is Lafayette College in Easton, Pennsylvania. It was established in 1826, before Lafayette's death. The college's founding fathers had not originally planned to honor Lafayette. They simply wanted to build a school to educate the children of Easton. However, this changed when Lafayette returned to the United States for his 1824–1825 tour. The people hoped Lafayette would come to visit them. Easton did not make it onto Lafayette's tour schedule. The people decided to go to him instead. A group of about two hundred citizens traveled to Philadelphia to hear Lafayette speak. It took the group two days to row down a river to see him. It took another two days to walk home after the visit. The people were very impressed by Lafayette. They returned to Easton wanting to name the college in his honor. Today, the college's library and archives house thousands of pieces of Lafayette memorabilia.

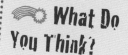

What Do You Think?

How do you define the word *hero*? What was it about Lafayette that made people admire him and want to pay tribute to his memory?

Ramer History House sits at the heart of Lafayette College in Easton, Pennsylvania. The college was named in celebration of the Marquis de Lafayette

GLOSSARY

abundance plenty, more than enough

artillery a military division that uses rifles and muskets as their primary weapon

bankruptcy a legal state in which property is seized in order to pay debts; inability to pay debts

blockade a military tactic in which ships prevent supplies from reaching a city or blockaded area

cadet a student in military training

cargo the goods carried by a ship or vessel

civil rights the rights to participate in government and society, usually voting

colonies settlements controlled by a mother country and settled by immigrants

commission a position as a military officer

commoners people not from the noble class; ordinary people

compensation money in exchange for work or an action; salary or payment

delegate people elected to a congress or group to act for the people

depose to remove an official or monarch from office or throne

disband to break up or leave

economic having to do with the exchange of money or goods

enlisted volunteered or signed up for the military; not commissioned into an officer position

equality being equal, or not changing from one person to another

eulogy a speech given in honor of someone; usually at funerals

exile having to leave one's country or home

Freemason member of the brotherhood of Masons, a secret organization

furlough permission to leave for a set period of time

gentleman farmer someone who farms or owns a farm for amusement; a farmer who does not need to make a living from his or her farm

impeach to charge a public official with a crime or improper behavior

Intolerable Acts acts passed by British Parliament to tax American colonies

Loyalists colonists who were loyal to Great Britain and King George III

monarch the king or queen; during the American Revolution, George III was king of Great Britain, Louis XVI was king of France

nobleman a member of a noble family, often distantly related to the monarch

novel a printed book that is an extended work of fiction

Patriots American colonists who wanted more rights or even independence from Great Britain

peace treaty an agreement signed by two or more nations to end a war

peasants workers and laborers

peninsula land surrounded by water on three sides

precarious dangerous, likely to fall into a bad situation

quarters living area

radical a person or idea which is far from the accepted norm

Redcoats a nickname for British soldiers, from the red uniform coats

redoubts a small fortification or stronghold

regiment a military unit made up of several battalions, usually several hundred soldiers

repeal to retract or cancel, usually a law

retroactively to do after an event or fact

representative government a government which is run by people elected by the nation

seize to take by force

Seven Years' War a conflict between France and Great Britain; fought in North America, Europe, and East Asia

skirmish a small battle or fight

stir a disturbance or well-known discussion

surrender to give up or stop fighting

temporarily only for the mean time

terrain land, usually rocky or difficult

traitor a citizen who betrays his or her country or homeland

treason betraying one's nation or country

TIMELINE

1757	*September 6*	Marie-Joseph Paul Yves Roch Gilbert du Motier Lafayette is born
1769		Lafayette orphaned
1771		Lafayette joins Black Musketeers
1773	*December 16*	Boston Tea Party
1774		Lafayette marries Adrienne de Noailles
	September 5	First Continental Congress
1775		Lafayette joins the Freemasons
	April 19	Battle of Lexington; American Revolution begins
1776	*July 4*	Declaration of Independence
	September	Silas Deane is sent to France as a commissioner
1777	*Spring*	*La Victoire* sets sail
	June	Lafayette arrives in North Carolina
	July	Lafayette becomes youngest Major General in the Continental Army
	September 11	Lafayette wounded at Battle of Brandywine
1778	*May 20*	Battle of Barren Hill
	June 28	Battle of Monmouth
	Late September	Benedict Arnold disappears
1781	*October 19*	Battle of Yorktown
1782		Lafayette returns to France
1789		Lafayette writes the *Declaration of the Rights of Man and of the Citizen*; French Revolution begins; Lafayette becomes Commander of the National Guard
1792		French Assembly declares war on Austria; King Louis XVI is deposed; Lafayette impeached and later imprisoned
1794		Adrienne is imprisoned
1795		Adrienne is released
1797		Lafayette is released
1824	*August 15*	Lafayette arrives in Staten Island
	August 24	Lafayette visits Boston
	September 28	Lafayette visits Philadelphia
	October 2	Lafayette visits Washington, D.C.
	October 17	Lafayette visits Mount Vernon
1825	*May 3*	Lafayette visits Nashville
	July 26	Lafayette visits Brandywine
	September 8	Lafayette departs for France
1826		Lafayette College established in Easton, Pennsylvania
1834	*May 20*	Lafayette dies

FURTHER READING AND WEBSITES

Books

Aloian, Molly. *George Washington: Hero of the American Revolution*. Crabtree Publishing Company, 2013.

Aloian, Molly. *Phillis Wheatley: Poet of the Revolutionary Era*. Crabtree Publishing Company, 2013.

Clarke, Gordon. *Significant Battles of the American Revolution*. Crabtree Publishing Company, 2013.

Mason, Helen. *Life on the Homefront during the American Revolution*. Crabtree Publishing Company, 2013.

Maestro, Betsy. *Liberty or Death: The American Revolution: 1763-1783*. Harper Collins, 2005.

Payan, Gregory. *Marquis de Lafayette: French Hero of the American Revolution*. Rosen: 2002.

Perritano, John. *The Causes of the American Revolution*. Crabtree Publishing Company, 2013.

Perritano, John. *The Outcome of the American Revolution*. Crabtree Publishing Company, 2013.

Roberts, Steve. *King George III: England's Struggle to Keep America*. Crabtree Publishing Company, 2013.

Websites

"Château Lafayette."
http://www.chateau-lafayette.com/-rubrique29-.html

"Heroes of the Revolution."
http://library.thinkquest.org/11683/heroes.html

"Marquis de Lafayette."
http://www.monticello.org/site/jefferson/marquis-de-lafayette

"The Marquis de Lafayette."
http://www.history.org/almanack/people/bios/biolafayette.cfm

"Who Served Here?: The Marquis de Lafayette."
http://www.ushistory.org/valleyforge/served/lafayette.html

BIBLIOGRAPHY

Books

America: History of Our Nation. Pearson Prentice Hall, 2007.

Bernier, Oliver. *Lafayette: Hero of Two Worlds.* E.P. Dutton, Inc., 1983.

Clary, David A. *Adopted Son: Washington, Lafayette, and the Friendship That Saved the Revolution;* Bantam Books, 2007.

Furneaux, Rupert. *The Pictorial History of the American Revolution.* J. G. Ferguson Publishing, 1973.

Gaines, James R. *For Liberty and Glory.* W.W. Norton & Company, 2007.

Gottschalk, Louis. *Lafayette Joins the American Army.* The University of Chicago Press, 1974.

Gottschalk, Louis and Margaret Maddox. *Lafayette in the French Revolution: Through the October Days.* The University of Chicago Press, 1969.

History of the American Revolution. American Heritage Inc., 2003.

Idzerda, Stanley J. and Loveland and Miller. *Lafayette, Hero of Two Worlds: The Art and Pageantry of His Farewell Tour of America. 1824–1825;* The Queen's Museum, 1989.

Kramer, Lloyd. *Lafayette in Two Worlds: Public Cultures and Private Identities in an Age of Revolutions.* University of North Carolina Press, 1996.

Lane, Jason. *General and Madame de Lafayette: Partners in Liberty's Cause in the American and French Revolutions.* Taylor, 2003.

Meister, Charles W. *The Founding Fathers.* McFarland & Company, 1987.

Unger, Harlow Giles. *Lafayette.* Wiley, 2003.

Websites

"The Battle of Minden." British Battles.com, 2012.
http://www.britishbattles.com/seven-years/minden.htm

Gascoigne, Bamber ."The History of the French Revolution." History of the World, Online; 2001.
http://www.historyworld.net/wrldhis/plaintexthistories.asp?historyid=ac04

Lafayette, Marquis de. "Declaration of the Rights of Man – 1789." The Avalon Project, Lillian Goldman Law Library, Yale Law School, 2008.
http://avalon.law.yale.edu/18th_century/rightsof.asp

"Louis XVI Biography." A & E Television Networks, Online, 2012.
http://www.biography.com/people/louis-xvi-9386943?page=1

"Marie Antoinette and the French Revolution." David Grubin Productions Inc., Online, 2006.
http://www.pbs.org/marieantoinette/faces/louis_xvi.html

"Marie Antoinette and the French Revolution: Reign of Terror: 1793–1794." David Grubin Productions Inc., Online, 2006.
http://www.pbs.org/marieantoinette/timeline/reign.html

"Marquis de Lafayette." Thomas Jefferson Encyclopedia, Online, 2012.
www.monticello.org/site/jefferson/marquis-de-lafayette

"The Marquis de Lafayette." National Center for the American Revolution/Valley Forge Historical Society, Online, 2011.
www.ushistory.org/valleyforge/served/lafayette.html

"The Marquis de Lafayette." New York City Statues, 2009.
http://newyorkcitystatues.com/mdl-inprospect-park/

INDEX